Original title:
Fruitful Moments

Copyright © 2025 Creative Arts Management OÜ
All rights reserved.

Author: Tobias Sterling
ISBN HARDBACK: 978-1-80586-460-8
ISBN PAPERBACK: 978-1-80586-932-0

Starlit Gatherings

Under the twinkling lights we dance,
A banana slipped, oh what a chance!
Juggling apples with little care,
One falls into dad's thick hair.

Cherries giggle, round and bright,
Even lemons join the flight.
Grapes are bouncing all around,
As we roll on the silly ground.

Plums start a conga, what's the deal?
Even oranges twirl, just to feel.
A watermelon thought it could sing,
But got stuck, that silly thing!

With maraschino hats we cheer,
To the funniest fruit of the year.
So grab a peach, let laughter flow,
In our starlit gathering's glow.

The Heart's Orchard

In the heart's orchard, where laughter grows,
Pears wear glasses, as everyone knows.
A picnic of puns under leafy shade,
An apple joke? Well, that one's played!

Strawberries plot with their sweet little schemes,
Throwing bright berries into our dreams.
A lemon slipped on a zesty lime,
Falling while rehearsing a fruit mime!

Peaches gossip, fluffed up with cream,
Boys teasing the boys, or so it would seem.
Raspberries snicker, while melons sway,
Creating a ruckus, come join the play!

As cherries chuckle, we start to race,
All in the orchard, a wild embrace.
With silly fruit antics, a party anew,
In this heart's orchard, there's fun to pursue!

Lush Journeys Through the Heart

On a sunny day, I felt quite swell,
A banana slipped; oh, what a yell!
Tumbling down with a pie in hand,
I rolled like fruit, it was simply grand.

Mangoes giggled in the afternoon light,
Juggling oranges, a comical sight.
Lemons laughed as they rolled away,
Squeezing joy through the lemony play.

Seeds of Tomorrow

Planting seeds in socks, what a thrill,
Socks sprouting blooms gave quite a chill.
Watering them, I wore a hat,
Fashion faux pas? Nah, quirky is that!

Peas in pockets, a tasty delight,
A butterfly landed, oh what a sight!
Bouncing beans hopping out to dance,
Their joyful leaps put my heart in a trance.

Harvested Whispers

Whispers in the orchard, berries conspired,
Telling secrets of pies they desired.
With a giggle, they plopped in a bowl,
Winking at me, they stirred up my soul.

The apple's a joker, a prankster supreme,
Spinning tales of a wildest dream.
Peaches chuckled as they danced around,
Fruits in a frolic, a sweet, silly sound.

Echoes of Abundance

Echoes of laughter float through the trees,
Grapes in a bunch whisper jokes with ease.
Strawberries burst into giggles of zest,
Rhubarb just shook, it knew it was best.

Bananas were boasting of their funny peel,
Apples chimed in with their crunchy appeal.
With cherries conversing, their voices combined,
A fruit-filled hullabaloo, joyfully designed.

Petal-Powered Dreams

In the garden soft and bright,
Flowers giggle in the light.
Bees are buzzing, having fun,
Chasing petals on the run.

Dandelions wearing crowns,
Twist and twirl, but never frown.
Ladybugs dance a jig so grand,
A flower band across the land.

Memories in Bloom

In the orchard, apples sway,
"Pick me first!" they shout, hooray!
Bananas slip and laugh aloud,
While cherries cheer, quite proud.

Peaches blush in the morning sun,
Every bite is purest fun.
Baskets full, a tasty spree,
Nature's joke, just wait and see.

Citrus-Spiced Adventures

Oranges rolling down the lane,
Citrus smiles and little rain.
Lemons squirt with playful glee,
Sour faces, oh, whee!

Limes are giggling on the vine,
Making jokes, oh so divine!
Grapefruit winks, "Oh, what a scene!",
Squeezing laughter, pure and clean.

Resplendent Reflections

In the market, colors burst,
Strawberries lead the merry thrust.
Ripe and red, they tease and boast,
While kiwi sings the sweetest toast.

Melons giggle, yellow and green,
Fruits unite for a wacky scene.
Juicy chaos fills the air,
Laughing til we all declare!

Orchard Trails

In the orchard where apples play,
I tripped on a banana today.
Squirrels giggled, oh what a sight,
As I danced with fruit in delight.

Peaches rolled like tiny balls,
Tomatoes made their slippery calls.
Chasing cherries, all round and red,
I tripped again, oh please, not my head!

Even the pears were having fun,
They whispered jokes, one by one.
With every slip, I'd laugh and gleam,
In this fruity, nutty dream!

With laughter echoing up in the trees,
Came bees buzzing, swirling like a breeze.
Caught in the chaos, my shoes did squeak,
But my heart was light, just take a peek!

The Warmth of Gathering

Gather 'round for a fruity feast,
With berries bright and pastries increased.
Grandpa's grinning, he's lost his hat,
Blaming it on a playful cat!

Cousins stack oranges in a heap,
Pineapples roll; oh, watch your leap!
A watermelon splatters, oh what a sight,
Everyone laughs, pure delight!

A cake made of cherries, a pie on a stand,
Uncle Joe's making his famous jam hand!
A tug on the table, round goes the chair,
Careful now, don't break the heirloom ware!

As laughter and food fill the afternoon,
A banana peel slips like a cartoon.
Nature's banquet, in colorful glee,
Who knew family gatherings would be so fruity?

Tantalizing Tides of Time

Time drifts like grapes in a bowl,
With tick-tock laughter, oh how we roll!
A lemon slice dances under the sun,
As we giggle at life, making every run.

The clock strikes one, it's time for pie,
But there's a fruit fight lurking nearby.
Strawberries fly, a raspberry bomb,
Who knew dessert could feel like a con!

Nourished by Nature

In gardens bright, where veggies snack,
Carrots converse, but watch your back!
Tomatoes chuckle from vine to vine,
"Oh look at that—unripe wine!"

Sunflowers sway, silly and tall,
Whispering secrets, giggling for all.
Bees buzz by with a funny hum,
"Don't squash the squash, it's not a drum!"

With every sprout, a giggle grows,
Nature's humor, oh how it flows!
In this zany garden, so bright and fair,
We nourish our joy with love and care!

Moments Like Ripe Pears

In the orchard, kids run fast,
Chasing shadows that never last.
Laughter spills like juice in sun,
Each bite a giggle, oh what fun!

Pears like treasures, sweet and round,
Squished underfoot, then rolling down.
We race to catch the fall parade,
With silly faces, total charade!

Honeyed Reflections

Sticky fingers, honey's got a grip,
On our cheeks, it takes a trip.
We watch the bees, they make a fuss,
While we snack and sip on bushels of us!

Sticky notes of sweet delight,
Scribbled thoughts, in the warm sunlight.
Do not eat the flowers! wise words read,
As petals form the fanciest spread!

Nature's Generosity

Bouncing balls of cherries bright,
Tossing them with all our might.
They land and prompt a wild cheer,
As birds start clapping, oh dear, oh dear!

"The tree just sneezed!" one yells with glee,
As apples tumble down the spree.
Gathered crumbs, a picnic feast,
With squirrels eyeing, a curious beast!

Essence of the Orchard

Saplings giggle, roots entwined,
They whisper secrets, now aligned.
"Pick me first!" a peach does pout,
While mischief brews along the route!

Juicy tales from vines, they weave,
A tale of fruit reclaiming eve.
As sunlight spritzes laughter's tease,
We dance beneath the boughs with ease!

Hues of Happiness

In the garden, ants do waltz,
Hidden treasures, no one faults.
Tomatoes giggle in their red,
Lettuce whispers, 'Let's go fed!'

Pumpkins chuckle with great mirth,
On their orange, a bit of worth.
Carrots hide beneath the ground,
'Only rabbits!' is their sound.

Squirrels propose a nutty dance,
In this twilight, give it a chance.
Berries blush with cheeky grace,
To compliment the sun's embrace.

Life's a puzzle, fruits entangled,
In laughter, smiles are wrangled.
With each harvest, joy's reprieve,
In silliness, we all believe.

Growing Through the Seasons

Springtime sprouts with giggles bright,
Blossoms nodding, pure delight.
Buds puff up like little pillows,
Hiding secrets with the willows.

Summer sun beams, a wild toast,
Peaches ripen, they boast the most.
Watermelons roll like clowns,
While berries climb in leafy gowns.

Autumn arrives with a funky beat,
Pumpkins frolic on their seat.
Crisp air brings a joyous crush,
As cider flows with a happy rush.

Winter whispers, 'Not so fast!'
Fruits can linger, memories vast.
In every season, fun is found,
As laughter echoes all around.

The Symphony of Ripeness

In orchards ripe, the fruits compose,
A symphony that grows and grows.
Apples wink with every swell,
As nature hums a jiggly bell.

Bananas dance, they slip and slide,
Mangoes tease, take joy with pride.
Limes are sour, but full of sass,
While cherries join in, jigging fast.

Ripe and round, the grapes do sing,
'To life, to joy, the fun we bring!'
With every bite, a laugh it steals,
As sweetness rolls in funny feels.

Orchestrated chaos, taste the sound,
In this fruitful jest, joy is found.
So twirl and whirl, come take a chance,
Life's a cheeky, tasty dance!

Cider and Sunlight

Underneath the cider tree,
Sunshine giggles, feeling free.
Jugs of joy, they bubble wide,
As bees buzz in a happy ride.

Apples tumble, hear them cheer,
Frogs join in, they croak sincere.
With every splash of golden drink,
Laughter flows, we smile and wink.

Clouds float by like cotton fluff,
Even time feels just enough.
Party hats upon the cask,
A fruity feast, no need to ask.

Raise a glass, let's toast the day,
As nature leads this grand ballet.
With cider sweet and sunlight bright,
We dance and laugh all through the night.

Sweetness in the Breeze

In the garden, apples lay,
Chasing bees, they frolic and play.
Lemons laughing in the sun,
Who knew cartwheels could be fun?

Ripe bananas swing on high,
Seeking clouds to steal the sky.
Peaches try to spin and dance,
While strawberries join in the prance.

Cherries giggle in their red,
Pitting courage in their head.
Grapes all burst into a cheer,
Mirth and laughter, oh so near!

In this patch of fruity cheer,
Every moment brings a tear.
With a wink and silly smile,
Life's a feast that's worth our while!

The Blooming Hour

A melon sings a silly tune,
Underneath the glowing moon.
Carrots join in with a jig,
While veggies hug, feeling big!

Tomatoes blush in summer's light,
As they dance with pure delight.
Radishes roll in muddy glee,
Waving hands, 'Come laugh with me!'

Onions grin with layers wide,
Stirring laughter, won't they slide?
Zucchini murmur silly rhymes,
All around, the joy just climbs.

In this circle, mirth does grow,
Fruits and veggies steal the show.
As petals drop, the laughter soars,
Blooming joy is what restores!

Juicy Revelations

A kiwi speaks, "I've got the scoop,
I once joined a silly fruit troupe!"
Lemonheads bobbed in laughter's glee,
Sipping tea under the peach tree.

Pineapples wear their crowns with pride,
Hula dancing, they won't hide.
Watermelon laughs, "I'm the boss,
Just don't call me a big green loss!"

Berries burst with secrets sweet,
Spilling whispers, oh what a treat!
Grapes in line, a tangled mess,
"Who knew that chaos could impress?"

Each juicy tale, a twist of fate,
Fruits unite, it's never late.
In this frenzy, smiles ignite,
Juicy fun, oh what a sight!

Nectar of the Soul

In a world where fruit does sing,
Mangoes bring the joy of spring.
Avocados joke, so creamy smooth,
Making guacamole in a groove.

Figs gossip under leafy shade,
Spreading stories, not afraid.
Papayas wink with sunset hues,
Inviting all to share their views.

Coconuts roll without a care,
Playing tag in coastal air.
Pomegranates take the stage,
Seeded laughter, all the rage!

Nectar flows, it lifts us high,
In this realm, we laugh and fly.
Sweet delights will never tire,
This fruity life ignites desire!

Sowing Seeds of Contentment

In my garden, I did stand,
With seeds aplenty in my hand.
I tripped over a pesky vine,
And landed hard—now I'm a swine!

The veggies sprouted all around,
But where's the lettuce? It ain't found!
A rabbit munches with a grin,
While I just splash in mud—oh, win!

The carrots giggle, they won't share,
With squishy boots and messy hair.
I wave my arms like crazy mad,
Each plant just laughs—my luck's so bad!

Yet in this chaos of my plot,
I plant my dreams and tie the knot.
Amidst the weeds, I find my cheer,
For laughter grows me, year by year!

Melodies of the Harvest

I whistled tunes while picking fruit,
But stumbled on a big ol' root.
An apple hit me on the head,
And now I'm seeing colors red!

The pears are dancing in a line,
While plums make jokes—oh, they're divine!
The oranges are rolling away,
And lemons joining in the play!

With every basket I shall fill,
The berries giggle, what a thrill!
I joke with grapes, they laugh in bunches,
As I enjoy delightful crunches.

So here's a toast to silly fruit,
Their funny ways don't give a hoot.
I'll dance with joy among the vines,
In this sweet chaos, life just shines!

Whispers Among the Leaves

The trees conspire with each breeze,
Their laughing whispers tease and tease.
A squirrel slips in fruit-filled glee,
And drops a peach right onto me!

The apples are gossiping quite loud,
While bananas form a jungle crowd.
The pumpkins chuckle at my shoes,
As I slip on a patch of goo!

So I embrace this leafy jest,
With every fruit, I find the best.
I'm dodging raindrops, dancing free,
While nature's pranks just make me squeal!

In this wild garden full of sound,
It's joy and laughter all around.
The fruits and leaves with playful cheer,
Bring silly moments, year by year!

The Gathering of Sweetness

The picnic's set with fruits galore,
Strawberries stacked high, what a score!
But as I reach for that sweet pie,
A seagull swoops, oh me, oh my!

With laughter ringing in the air,
I chase that bird without a care.
But tripped on jelly, what a sight,
I landed in a fruit-filled fight!

The melons roll, and cherries fly,
As friends all laugh, we wonder why.
This messy spread, a sight so fine,
Turns into chaos—party divine!

A shout rings out! "Let's have some fun!"
As fruit salads become a run.
With laughter shared, we all agree,
In fruity mayhem, life's the key!

Orchard Chatter

In the orchard, apples play,
Running races, day by day.
Peaches giggle, what a sight,
Bouncing high, in sheer delight.

Grapes roll out to steal some sun,
While cherries hide, just for fun.
A pear gets stuck on a tree limb,
Declaring boldly, it won't be dim!

Each fruit's gossip fills the air,
Bananas dance without a care.
Lemons pucker, make a face,
While figs just laugh, in joyful grace.

Come and join this playful crew,
Sharing tales of things they do.
In the orchard, joy's the key,
Where every fruit's a comedy!

Harvesting Laughter

In fields abloom, the pumpkins prance,
While zucchini's gone for quite a dance.
Tomatoes tumble, red with glee,
And corn stands tall to host a spree.

Carrots dig in just to play,
Shouting loudly, 'We're here to stay!'
Radishes poke fun at the peas,
While cucumbers chill in the breeze.

Sunflowers whisper, stories told,
Of a harvest bright and bold.
With laughter ringing through the rows,
Each veggie boasts in fun-filled shows.

Come and reap the joy we stitch,
In every laugh, there's quite a pitch.
Harvesting smiles is our great art,
With every joke, we truly part!

Fern-Flecked Memories

In the woods where ferns are grand,
Mushrooms giggle at their stand.
Squirrels chatter, tails of fluff,
In this green place, we get enough.

Raccoons steal snacks, oh what a crime,
While owls hoot, 'Ain't it prime?'
Berries blushing, all aglow,
Chortle softly, 'Let's take it slow.'

Dancing leaves share silly news,
As shadows hide from playful views.
In this space, where laughter springs,
Memories grow like tiny things.

Join the merry fern-filled scene,
Where thoughts are light, and minds serene.
In this patch, we find our cheer,
With every giggle, year by year!

The Spice of Life's Lessons

In kitchens bright, the spices play,
Cinnamon twirls, while pepper says, 'Hey!'
Garlic laughs as it stirs the pot,
Chili peppers bring the heat, a lot!

Basil winks with a sprig so green,
While thyme narrates a cooking scene.
Oregano's jokes, they never fade,
As sage advises, 'Don't be afraid!'

Nutmeg chimes in with a giggle of zest,
Saying cooking lessons are simply the best.
In this hot spot, joy takes flight,
Every blend brings pure delight.

Join the banquet where fun resides,
With every sprinkle, laughter hides.
The spice of life, it surely shines,
In every dish, where humor aligns!

Gardens of Delight

In a garden where the gnomes play,
Pumpkins dance and carrots sway.
Lettuce laughs with leafy cheer,
While radishes roast, oh my dear!

A gopher pops his head at night,
Chasing fireflies that take flight.
Tomato jokes that split the seams,
While peas share all their silly dreams.

But watch your step, don't lose your shoes,
For cabbage rolls are known to snooze.
Garden tools with minds of their own,
Trowels laugh, "You're not alone!"

When harvest comes and all's in bloom,
Squash puns echo in the room.
A feast of laughter on each plate,
In this verdant world, can't hesitate!

When Time Bears Fruit

A clock tick-tocks with fruity flair,
Bananas grinning, breezy air.
Time plays pranks and spins quite fast,
Like peaches slipping, nothing lasts.

A grapevine chit-chatting away,
Says "Lime is sour, but what a play!"
Cherries giggle in a tight bunch,
While apples tease with swords to munch.

When seconds pause, the berries cheer,
For jelly beans commandeer the sphere.
Bring out the pies, let laughter spread,
While cupcakes bow and nod their heads.

So grab your fruit, let banter flow,
With every slice, the giggles grow.
In this orchard of humor ripe,
Life's tasting sweet, oh take a bite!

Bounty in the Shadows

In twilight's grasp, where shadows play,
Mushrooms chuckle at the end of day.
Radishes don capes, oh so grand,
While shadows tickle a veggie band.

Tomatoes blush under leafy caps,
As hidden bounty sings and claps.
Carrots whisper secret tales,
Of moonlit gardens and veggie trails.

Beets tell tales of the earth beneath,
While onions share their layered grief.
In this twilight bazaar of art,
The sweetest laughs are set apart.

So join the harvest, share a jest,
In shadows deep, the fun's the best.
With every bite, the giggles loom,
In this garden, laughter's in full bloom!

Vines of Connection

Twisting tales from vine to vine,
Sun-kissed squash say, "Isn't it fine?"
With roots entwined, they plot and scheme,
Creating laughter like a dream.

Cucumbers roll on the garden floor,
"Oh leafy friend, let's ask for more!"
The grapevines nod, "Is it time to play?"
As zucchinis cheer on the merry fray.

Here in the rows, the laughter's thick,
Beetroot jokes land like a brick.
With every twirl, they chuckle and sway,
Making each other giggle all day.

So join the dance, bring in your wit,
In this vine-tangled joy, never quit.
For in each laugh, the colors ignite,
Connecting all under the moonlight!

Ripeness of the Heart

In the orchard where giggles grow,
Love's ripe laughter steals the show.
Each hug's a peach, each kiss a pear,
Sweet moments hang in the warm air.

Tickles abound like fruit on trees,
I trip on joy like it's a breeze.
With every smile, the harvest's bright,
My heart's a feast day and night.

We juggle dreams like oranges round,
In this silly circus, joy is found.
Bouncing ideas like bouncing balls,
Laughter echoes through the halls.

So let's gather 'round, let's munch and crunch,
On moments shared—oh, what a brunch!
With every bite, let's swish and sway,
In our fruity hearts, we'll always play.

Banquet of Memories

At a table set with jam and fun,
We reminisce until we run.
Each dish a tale, each sip a cheer,
Banana bread dreams, let's dive into gear!

The punch bowl flows with stories bright,
Avocado whispers, oh what a sight!
We toast to moments that bring delight,
Like berries bursting in morning light.

Peas in a pod with laughter's grace,
Carrot-top wigs, what a silly race!
With every bite of joy we take,
This banquet of memories won't break.

So grab a fork, or just your hands,
Dive into laughter, make your plans.
In this feast of joy, the smiles expand,
With each silly joke, we take a stand.

Time's Plentiful Offering

Time's a vending machine of dreams,
Press the buttons, hear the screams!
Out pops a giggle, a wink, a smile,
Grab them quick; they're worth your while.

Each minute's ripe like juicy prunes,
Moments burst like bright balloons.
Tick-tock dances with a twist,
Sing along; you won't want to miss!

Sandwiches of laughter piled so high,
With a side of pie—oh my, oh my!
Seconds keep ticking, but who is counting?
Joy, like a fruit tree, keeps surmounting.

So munch on dreams, let giggles soar,
In this timing-game, we'll explore.
The clock may tick, but hearts will race,
And in this feast, we've found our place.

Colors of Tomorrow

Tomorrow comes like a fruit parade,
With colors splashed that won't fade.
An orange giggle, a purple cheer,
In this funny carnival, we won't steer clear!

Painting futures in silly hues,
Life's a canvas with vibrant views.
Yellow rays of laughter shine,
Join the circus, it's all divine!

Like strawberries bouncing in the sun,
Each day's an adventure, oh so fun!
Wrap me in colors, frilly and bold,
These precious moments are pure gold.

So toss your worries, let them roam,
With bursts of laughter, we'll find our home.
In this fruity festival of glee,
Tomorrow's waiting for you and me.

Beneath the Canopy of Dreams

Under trees, so wide and green,
Squirrels dance, a sight unseen.
Lemonade flows, a sweet delight,
We laugh and munch till late at night.

Picnic ants march in a line,
Stealing crumbs, oh! How they're fine.
We dodge them like a game of tags,
With laughter loud, and silly jags.

Shade from sun, a cozy place,
With watermelon, we make a race.
A seed-spitting contest starts with glee,
Who knew spitting could be so free?

The breeze tells jokes, it's quite a hoot,
Tickles our noses, brings out the fruit.
So underneath this leafy dome,
We find a world that feels like home.

The Flavor of Freedom

A peach so ripe, it rolls away,
Chasing it turns into a play.
Laughter echoes down the lane,
Where juice drips down, we're all insane.

We're pirates on a fruit-filled quest,
With grapes as treasure, we are blessed.
A cherry's smile, a juicy prank,
In our laughter, we'll fill the tank.

Fruits of freedom, in our hands,
Who needs solid, when we have lands?
With fruit hats, we dance around,
Joy in colors, pure and profound.

Bananas swing from every tree,
Making monkeys feel so free.
So come and join, let's share this bliss,
In every bite, there's a funny twist.

When Time Ripens

Time ticks slow when nectar's high,
A mango slips and starts to fly.
Falling softly with a thud,
The race begins, 'till we're back in mud!

We glance at clocks, then ignore,
As berries bounce and roll on floor.
A berry battle, oh what fun,
We wage this war until we run.

With laughter loud, we take our stand,
Holding fruit like a sword in hand.
Juice splatters on our silly dress,
Who needs shirts when we can mess?

Time may pass, but who will care?
In every munch, adventures share.
With fruits as friends, we'll dance and wander,
In laughter's hold, we fly like thunder.

Chasing the Golden Light

Chasing beams through leafy lanes,
A zesty orange slips down, it gains.
Rolling quick, it leads the race,
We dash behind with berry face.

Strawberries giggle in the sun,
Hearts are light, joy has begun.
With every bite, a quirky cheer,
A riot of pumpkin spice near.

Golden glow from trees above,
Dancing fruit, oh what a love!
We leap and twirl, in playful fight,
Chasing dreams in golden light.

With each splash and juicy fight,
Together we laugh till the night.
Memories made beneath this shine,
In every moment, joy is divine.

Petals and Pulp

In the garden where the berries swing,
The gnomes dance and the rainbows sing.
Watermelons joking, spilling their seeds,
While the sunflowers plot their leafy deeds.

Bees in tuxedos, buzzing with flair,
Chasing the daisies, unaware of the air.
Lemons with laughter, tangy and bright,
Rolling off tables, oh what a sight!

Cherry pies giggle, adding to the fun,
While cucumbers debate who's the punniest one.
The apples just wink, feeling quite sly,
As pumpkins recite their old rhymes on the fly.

In this orchard of laughter, the fruits hold sway,
With chuckles and chuckles, they frolic and play.
Petals and pulp, a comical mix,
In the world of the funny, they're the best tricks.

Bounty Beneath the Branches

Under branches where the coconuts chill,
A squirrel in shades works on his skill.
Papayas proclaim they're the life of the feast,
While kumquats gather, joy never ceased.

Grapes play charades, rolling on vines,
While figs chat secrets, sipping on pines.
Oranges joke about running away,
Sneaking a dance with the sun's golden ray.

Kiwi with laughter, all fuzzy and bright,
Challenges bananas to a slip-and-slide fight.
Underneath laughter, the fruits start to gleam,
Bounty beneath branches is a whimsical dream.

Each fruit has its quirk, a comical twist,
In this playful place, you'll never be missed.
With nature's own humor, the joy is immense,
In this sweet, silly world, it's great to commence.

Savoring the Seasons

In springtime's giggle, the berries appear,
Laughter and sweetness fill up the cheer.
Ants in tuxedos, marching in lines,
Savoring flavors as the sun brightly shines.

Summer's a party with peaches galore,
Watermelons crashing—oh, what a roar!
Mangoes are juggling, trying to be wise,
With coconuts cracking jokes that surprise.

Autumn arrives with its pumpkin pie,
While apples make cider, oh my, oh my!
Cranberries gossip, all tart yet sweet,
And nuts crack pun after nutty feat.

Winter rolls in with a frosty delight,
Oranges in scarves, oh, what a sight!
Savoring seasons, the fruits tell their tale,
In the laughter of nature, we all shall prevail.

Ripe Reflections

In the orchard of mirth, the fruits share their tales,
With giggles and winks, they chase off the gales.
Pineapples ponder what's next on the menu,
While peaches pluck ukuleles in the venue.

Watermelons whisper, their secrets so sweet,
"I'm juicing this moment, can't take a seat!"
Grapefruit grins widely, all zesty and bright,
While cherries play tag, in a colorful plight.

Ripe reflections bounce off the trees,
Bananas in sombreros dance in the breeze.
Kiwis in a conga, the figs won't be shy,
In a fruity fiesta, laughter fills the sky.

Under the stars, the flavors unite,
In this merry mingling, everything feels right.
With laughter that ripens, the fruits lead the way,
In the garden of joy, it's a sunny buffet!

Barrel of Delights

In a barrel filled with jolly jam,
Squeezed in tight like a fruity clam.
Rolling grapes and laughing pears,
Tumbling over without a care.

A peach with a grin, a plum with a joke,
Banana peels make everyone choke!
They dance on the rim, a silly show,
Who knew a barrel could steal the show?

The apples in there wear funny hats,
Chasing each other like acrobatic cats.
Fruits having fun, what a sight to see,
In this fruity circus, just let it be!

From a berry who sings to a cheeky lime,
Each giggle they share is simply sublime.
Together they frolic, so bright and spry,
In this barrel of laughs, oh me, oh my!

Aromas of Affection

In the kitchen, scents swirl like a dance,
Bananas in pajamas start a romance.
A loaf of bread flirts with some cheese,
While cinnamon rolls try to wheeze.

Garlic and onion exchanged glances,
With herbs that giggle as nature prances.
A tomato blushes, ripe and round,
While butter slides in without a sound.

Lemons roll in with a citrus cheer,
While strawberries giggle, 'We're all up here!'
In this fragrant fiesta of love and fun,
Amidst kitchen chaos, they dance as one.

So bring out the laughter, the spice, and zest,
In this aromatic party, we're surely blessed.
Every whiff a chuckle, every bite a jest,
In this happy kitchen, we're all guests!

The Berry-Picking Hour

Berry pickers with baskets in tow,
Wading through bushes all in a row.
The strawberries giggle, the blueberries squeal,
As pickers fumble, it's quite the deal.

Hats turn sideways, and shoes go askew,
One slips in mud—oh what a view!
Raspberries blush while the pickers all laugh,
'Looks like we've found nature's own photograph!'

A cherry rolls off, bouncing away,
A pickle's a fruit? Who made this play?
Laughter erupts as they chase the red,
With each little slip, a new prank is bred.

So on this bright day, with fruit in sight,
The berry-picking crew takes to flight.
For every berry they gather with cheer,
Comes tales of folly that all can hear!

Lasting Impressions

With every slice of that pie so sweet,
A cherry on top makes the day complete.
For every bite, there's a laughter-filled tale,
From the kitchen stage to the great big gale.

Pineapple rings laugh in the light,
While silly old oranges start a food fight.
"Peel me!" they giggle, "No, not today!"
As lemons roll off and dance away.

A squirrel swings by for a nibble or two,
"Watch where you're going!" they all shout, "Boo!"
When syrup spills over, it's sticky delight,
In this world of flavor, oh what a sight!

With teetering treats and shaky cheer,
In this banquet of smiles, all friends draw near.
Each morsel a memory, each chuckle a mark,
In the scrapbook of life, it's a bright, funny spark!

The Taste of Togetherness

We gathered round with snacks in hand,
A feast of laughter, oh so grand.
Bananas slipped and cherries bounced,
Each fruit-induced giggle, joy pronounced.

Peaches squished and jelly spilled,
On the table, chaos thrilled.
Grapes rolled off, a slippery crew,
In this fruity mess, friendships grew.

Strawberries winked; they knew their fate,
To be devoured, oh, it's great!
We toasted with lemonade in cheer,
These silly moments we hold dear.

The plates were empty, hearts were full,
Life tastes best when it's colorful.
In laughter's echo, we found our groove,
In every bite, our spirits move.

Sun-Kissed Reminiscence

Citrus scents danced in the sun,
Orange peels flew, oh, what fun!
We chased each other, sticky with juice,
In playful battles, we felt loose.

Lemonade rivers flowed from the stand,
Sipping sweet, we took a stand.
The ice cubes jiggled, making us smile,
While our laughter echoed for a mile.

A picnic spread, so bright and bold,
Fruit salads made our hearts unfold.
But ants arrived, oh what a scene,
Raiding our feast like a sneaky team!

As the sun dipped low, we sang with glee,
Every moment ripe as it could be.
With sticky fingers and tummy aches,
We promised, next time, to eat more cakes.

The Language of Growth

Planted seeds in our little patch,
We watered dreams with a little catch.
Talking to veggies, they seemed to grin,
Every sprout tells a tale within.

Pumpkins promised a spooky night,
While carrots tried to grow upright.
Zucchini peeked with a cheeky glance,
In this garden, we'd all dance.

Fruits wore hats made of leafy green,
Chucking dirt, the mess was seen.
We played pretend with fruits and roots,
Barefoot in soil, wearing mixed smiles and suits.

Under the stars, we tallied our cheer,
Each plant spoke a language clear.
With laughter and joy, we bloomed so bright,
In our garden, everything felt just right.

Abundant Reverie

In the orchard where giggles sway,
We climbed the trees and made our play.
Apples tumbled, landing with flair,
Creating giggles that filled the air.

Baskets teeming, we raced in glee,
Fruits flung high like a wild spree.
With pie on faces, we shared delight,
Under the stars, all felt just right.

Berry picking turned into a sport,
With sticky fingers, what a report!
Peaches blushed as we found them last,
Each moment together, a joyful blast.

As twilight fell, we toasted the day,
With fruity drinks, we'd laugh and sway.
In our tales of bounty and cheer,
These memories, oh, they'll persevere!

Wildberries and Wandering Souls

In the forest, a berry parade,
Dancing squirrels, joyfully swayed.
Berries burst, a sweet surprise,
Who knew fruit could wear such ties?

Chasing giggles, lost in the bloom,
Happiness ripen in nature's room.
Mischief brewed in a berry patch,
Life's punchline, with each little batch.

Spot a bear, oh what a sight!
He's munching berries, with pure delight.
But he snickers, as I run away,
Squirrels throw berries like a playful bouquet.

So we laugh in this fruity spree,
Berry juice stains, wild and free.
Nature's jest is the sweetest score,
In wild places, there's never a bore!

Nectar of Nostalgia

Memories drip like honey sweet,
Grandma's laughter, can't be beat.
Peach cobbler left on the sill,
Time to reminisce, what a thrill!

A picnic spread beneath the sky,
Sandwiches stacked, oh me, oh my!
Forgot the fruit? What a blunder,
A pass-the-peach game? Now that's a wonder!

The ants arrive, an uninvited crew,
But they bring stories of their own too.
Each share a taste of that sunlit day,
Oh how we savored our youthful play.

Laughter echoes in the afternoon,
Nectar of nostalgia, like a tune.
Every bite is a stroll down lane,
Where flavors linger, sweet and insane!

Colors of Abundance

With colors bright, the orchard gleams,
Pudding cups filled with fruity dreams.
Orange and red, a sight so grand,
Who needs a brush when you have a hand?

Plucking apples, we giggle and rush,
Belly-flops in a berry bush.
Grapes like jewels, so many to munch,
Watch out for stains—now that's a punch!

The fruit basket overflowed with cheer,
"Please no more!" I dramatically jeer.
Yet one more slice, so juicy and fine,
Each color bursting, a party divine.

As colors dance on our laughing tongues,
We sing with joy, our hearts are young.
Life's a carnival with each sweet bite,
In the orchard's bounty, all feels right!

Sunlit Journeys

Under the sun, we roam so free,
Orange peels tossed like confetti.
Every step sparked with playful glee,
Maps made of fruit, that's the key!

Lemon throws, a sour surprise,
Who's ducking now? Oh, what a rise!
Banana peels, a slippery twist,
Giggles echo, can't resist.

Ripe watermelon, a juicy treat,
Splashing juice is really quite neat.
Friends behind, we're racing the light,
Under the sky, everything feels bright.

Sunlit journeys with every taste,
Life's a feast, no time to waste!
With laughter shared, our hearts align,
Today's adventure is simply divine!

Petals and Promises

In a garden where daisies sway,
Bees dance like they own the day.
Tulips giggle in bright arrays,
Each petal whispers, "Come out and play!"

Chasing butterflies with glee,
Worms wiggle, plotting a spree.
Sunshine tickles the apple tree,
Where fruit drops down, just wait and see!

Rabbits munch on lettuce beds,
While squirrels wear their nutty threads.
Nature chuckles, joy ahead,
In this riot of greens and reds!

A cucumber sneezes, oh my!
Tomatoes blush as they spy.
In this patch, no room for shy,
Let's feast before the sun waves goodbye!

Savoring Sunlit Days

Picnics spread on checkered cloths,
Ants march in without an oath.
Lemonade spills as laughter froths,
While friends try not to explode with growth!

Watermelons take the stage,
Juggling slices, quite the rage.
Cantaloupe, a fruity sage,
Winks at pears, quite hard to gauge!

Kites go soaring in blue skies,
Like strawberries wearing ties.
Chasing shadows, oh the cries,
Warm days pass, how time flies!

As sun dips down, the fireflies shine,
Rhyme time with each sip of wine.
In this moment, life is divine,
With fruity giggles, all is fine!

The Orchard's Embrace

In the orchard, a chorus plays,
Apples blush in sunny rays.
Pies are baking, scent that sways,
While kiddos splash in fruit-filled bays!

Peaches pout, they think they're grand,
Grapes in clusters, hand in hand.
Cherries giggle, not so bland,
Discussing dreams, it's quite the stand!

Squirrels audition for a role,
As peaches plot a secret goal.
Underneath the old barn's whole,
Dance with joy, that's how we scroll!

Even ciders join the fun,
Making mischief on the run.
As the day begins to shun,
In the orchard, everyone's a pun!

Seasonal Serenade

Springtime brings the wildest schemes,
With fruit-tart kisses stealing dreams.
Bouncing berries burst at seams,
As lemon-lime concocts the beams!

Summer brings a golden glow,
Cucumber dances, don't you know?
Water balloons in a wild show,
All join in, putting on a toe!

Autumn whispers, time to bake,
With pumpkin pies and fruit fondake.
Silly apples start to quake,
As harvests dance, the world awakes!

Winter snuggles with a grin,
Fruits in sweaters, soft within.
Cozy tales of whimsy spin,
A seasonal joke, where laughs begin!

A Tapestry of Tastes

I met a pear, quite round and sweet,
It danced and twirled on tiny feet.
A lemon laughed, squeezed out some cheer,
While grapes all giggled, quite sincere.

A berry in a hat said, "Look at me!"
"I'm the juiciest of the berry spree!"
We made a punch, oh what a sight,
A fruit parade, a sheer delight!

Bananas slipped, did a funny fall,
Peaches rolled and bounced, a peachy ball.
In this wacky mix, we found our groove,
With every bite, we danced and moved.

This tasty shindig, oh such a bash,
With fruity friends, we made a splash!
So here's to laughter, zest, and cheer,
A feast of fun, let's spread the cheer!

Golden Hours in Greenery

The sun was bright, the grass was green,
We found a melon, fit for a queen.
It wore a crown of leafy crowns,
And sat upon our picnic grounds.

Tomatoes rolled like little balls,
While cucumbers danced down the walls.
A cabbage wore shades, looked quite cool,
In this garden party, we broke all rules!

We tried a dance with pears in tow,
But apples tumbled to say hello.
They giggled so much, they lost their peels,
In this quirky patch of giggling meals.

So here we toast with veggie cheer,
To golden hours we hold so dear.
And while we munch, let laughter roam,
In this green retreat, we found our home.

The Fruits of Togetherness

Under a tree, we all congregate,
With fruits so funny, it's a tasty fate.
A pineapple wore sunglasses, quite bold,
While cherries whispered secrets, still untold.

A coconut rolled and said, "Let me in!"
"I'm here for the party, let the fun begin!"
With berries bouncing, they formed a train,
Chasing each other down the lane.

We tossed a peach, it flew so high,
Smashing into grapes, oh my, oh my!
Laughter echoed as we gathered near,
These fruity pals made memories dear.

So here we are, a blended crew,
With every giggle, we start anew.
Together we shine, it's pure delight,
In this juicy tale, our hearts take flight.

A Canvas of Seasons

A canvas stretched with colors bright,
Fruits splashed joy, a merry sight.
Peppers painted red like sunsets glow,
While frost-kissed carrots put on a show.

Olive branches swayed with glee,
They clinked their glasses, wild and free.
Lemons juggled, a citrus act,
While oranges cheered, that's a fact!

As autumn leaves began to twirl,
Pineapples spun like a dancer's whirl.
In winter's chill, we'd roast and toast,
Sharing sweet moments, that's what we boast!

So paint your life with color and fun,
Savor the laughter, let joy run.
In every season, let spirits rise,
In this fruity play, we find our prize!

Echoing Abundance

In the kitchen, pots do sing,
Bananas leap, doing their fling.
Avocados roll, they think quite fast,
Peaches blush while having a blast.

Jelly jiggles, what a sight!
Grapes in dance, oh, what delight!
Skewers with fruit, a colorful play,
Mangoes cheer as they sway and sway.

Pineapples wear their crowns on high,
While lemons shout, 'Give it a try!'
Fruit flies buzz in silly parade,
Making mischief, all unafraid.

With laughter, the feast comes alive,
Every bite makes joy derive.
In this banquet, silly and bright,
The fruit of laughter takes its flight.

Blooms and Blessings

A strawberry waved from the vine,
Said, 'Hey there, I've got free wine!'
Cherries chuckled, swinging low,
Giggling all the way to the show.

Lemons in hats, looking quite fine,
Zestfully sippin' their citrus line.
Kiwi takes selfies with a big grin,
Snap, snap, snap, let the fun begin!

Mangoes jive with a tango flair,
Peanuts join in without a care.
Each one plays their unique part,
Creating laughter, warmth, and art.

In this garden, such a scene,
Where every berry wears a sheen.
Among the flowers, joy takes root,
Sow seeds of laughter, share the fruit!

Sparks of Sweetness

Berries burst like fireworks bright,
Fizzy drinks keep spirits light.
Pineapples wear their shades so cool,
While pears play hopscotch, breaking the rule.

Watermelons roll, a wobbly race,
Giggling grapes have made their place.
Sliced oranges cheer, what a crowd,
Fruit salad whispers, 'Please be loud!'

Melons spin in a zany dance,
Lime jokes leave you in a trance.
Bananas slip with style and flair,
In this circus, there's fun to spare.

Cheerful and bright, the table's set,
With each fruit joke, we laugh and fret.
In this sweetness, humor prevails,
Every slice tells the best of tales.

Tides of Generosity

Friendships bloom with figs and nuts,
Pomegranates roll, giving out hugs.
Citrus waves from trees with glee,
'Join us for a zesty spree!'

In a basket, apples take their turn,
Each one grinning, waiting to learn.
Plums gossip in a fruity spree,
Joking how fruit flies love free tea!

Berries bounce, on clouds they glide,
While melons float on the joy tide.
The sharing bowl, so full and round,
With laughter echoing all around.

At this banquet of cheerful cheer,
Friends find fruit and funny here.
Each bite, a giggle, a shared delight,
In this harvest, everything's right!

Melodies of Morning Dew

The sun creeps up with a sleepy yawn,
While snoozing cats on the lawn keep on.
Pancakes flip like a circus act,
And I wonder if syrup's a natural fact.

Birds chirp tunes that are off the beat,
While squirrels hold nutty gatherings neat.
A toast to toast, a jammed slice of bread,
Somehow the coffee spills on my head.

A worm does the tango in the soil,
While daisies laugh at the night's recoil.
I slip and slide on morning's dew,
With mismatched socks, there's much to pursue!

In this dance of dawn, my heart skips a thread,
For laughter blooms where the silliness spreads.
So let's cheer to the giggles, the rays, and the light,
For morning's mischief makes everything right.

Gardens of Gratitude

In the garden, weeds wear flower crowns,
As gophers dig in their underground towns.
I plant my seeds while chatting with bees,
They buzz with gossip beneath the trees.

Sunflowers stretch as if doing yoga,
While carrots compete in a veggie toga.
With earth on my nose and a smile so wide,
I chase after butterflies, giggling with pride.

The zucchini sneezes, what a silly sound,
While I watch my melon run circles around.
Each radish reveals a splash of delight,
In this garden where laughter takes flight.

We harvest smiles by the basketful,
In this patch where jokes are always full.
So let's plant joy in rows with finesse,
And sprinkle in laughter, oh what a mess!

Tasting the Twilight

As twilight settles with a wink and a nudge,
Fireflies flicker; I give them a grudge.
Eating popcorn while stars start to twinkle,
My dog thinks he's a star, but he only can sprinkle.

A picnic blanket's home to crumbs galore,
While sandwiches giggle as ants march and score.
Cucumbers sing as they lie in a bowl,
While lemonade pretends to be rock and roll.

The moon joins in with a silver glare,
While shadows compete for the laughter they share.
Chasing a breeze that steals my last fry,
Quips and jests in the cool evening sky.

What a feast of joy 'neath the verified stars,
With cosmic snacks that taste just like bars.
Let's munch on the dusk with hugs and delight,
In the zany dusk where everything's bright!

A Serenade to the Sun

Oh sun, you're a comedian in the sky,
With rays like jokes that just can't die.
You tickle my cheeks with a warm embrace,
While shadows bounce in a playful race.

Picnics abound with laughter in tow,
As ants form a band, putting on a show.
Chasing ice cream that melts on my leg,
I munch on a pickle, and then I beg!

To dance in the breeze, I grab my hat,
As squirrels join in, they're remarkably sprat.
Each sunflower winks, and what do I say?
'You're the sun's stand-up! Keep shining that way!'

With each golden ray, let the giggles grow,
A serenade of joy that's all in the flow.
So here's to the sun, a bright jester's smile,
In this wild summer, let's celebrate style!

In the Shade of Plenty

In the garden where laughter blooms,
Tomatoes grin, bursting with plumes.
Lemons giggle in bright yellow hues,
While peppers dance in their zesty shoes.

Pickles chuckle in jars of green,
Jellybeans rolling, oh what a scene!
Under the shade, the fruit has fun,
Even the apples are making a pun.

Peaches parade in their fuzzy coats,
While carrots trot in their juicy boats.
Berries bounce in a colorful race,
Each one vying for the silliest space.

So join the picnic, grab a plate,
It's a fruity party, don't be late!
With every bite, a giggle awaits,
In the shade where the fun never abates.

The Palette of Life

In the orchard, colors collide,
Fruits in shades of joy and pride.
Bananas, with their cheeky grins,
Telling tales of fruitastic wins.

Cherries blushing, up in a row,
Whispering secrets, soft and slow.
Kiwi, the jokester, with fuzzy flair,
Cracking jokes without a care.

Oranges spinning in a citrus dance,
Each one winking, taking a chance.
Grapes giggle as they tumble down,
Rolling their way to the juiciest town.

In this palette where humor reigns,
Colorful laughs are never in vain.
Life's sweetest moments, all combined,
In a fruity world, hilariously designed.

Moments on the Vine

On the vine where stories grow,
Laughter curls and zest flows,
Grapes, like comedians, hang so tight,
Each one crafting jokes at night.

Wine glasses toast to the fruity jest,
As berries burst, they giggle best.
Every sip, a ticklish delight,
Sparkling tales under the moonlight.

The sunbeams twinkle, laughing loud,
While cucumbers pose, ever proud.
The squash skedaddles away in a flash,
Sneaking in jokes with a happy bash.

Moments on the vine, oh what a treat,
With every taste, the humor's complete.
Join in the fun, raise your glass high,
In the vineyard where laughter can fly.

Blossoms of Gratitude

In gardens where giggles grow wild,
Peppers and onions play like a child.
Every sprout, a joke in disguise,
Blooming with laughter, oh what a prize!

Flowers wink with petal-y glee,
Sharing secrets with bumblebee.
Carrots strut in orange attire,
Chasing around in a veggie choir.

Radishes tease in their spunky red,
Telling stories of all that they fed.
Zucchinis play hide and seek, oh what fun,
With laughter echoing, all day run.

In this garden, joy fills the air,
Gratitude blossoms, everywhere.
So let's celebrate with fruit and cheer,
For every moment is precious here.

Colors of Gratitude

A tomato tried to dance in glee,
But slipped right off the countertop, you see.
Bananas giggled, 'What a sight!'
As we laughed and shared our fruity delight.

Grapes sang songs, in a funny way,
While apples rolled in a playful fray.
Pineapples wished for a hula dance,
And oranges squeezed out a ticklish chance.

Lemons made faces, quite a show,
Mangoes twirled to the rhythm slow.
With every laugh, our hearts grew wide,
In this colorful world where fruits abide.

The Gathering Place

In a bowl where the fruits convene,
Peaches and plums make quite the scene.
Berries gossip, sharing a jest,
While kiwis hide in their fluffy nest.

A watermelon dreamt of being a star,
But slipped on a peel, oh, how bizarre!
Pomegranates chuckled, seeds all aglow,
In this gathering, the laughter would flow.

Lemons played hopscotch, a citrus parade,
As pears teamed up for a comical charade.
With every chuckle, the fruit bowl swayed,
In this joyful place where memories stayed.

A Mosaic of Moments

Pineapples pranced in a patchwork dance,
While cherries giggled, taking a chance.
Fruits gathered close with a wink and a grin,
Creating a mosaic thick with kin.

Kiwis joked about their fuzzy façade,
While strawberries flashed their bright, bold charade.
In this silly world where laughter's a game,
Each moment a brushstroke, wild and untame.

Watermelons shouted, 'Let's make a scene!'
As they juggled fruits, vibrant and keen.
Every slice shared bore a laugh so grand,
In this mosaic, we all took a stand.

Savoring Every Slice

Cucumbers sliced while the sun did shine,
Causing giggles as they slipped down the line.
Pineapples winked, saying, 'Take it slow!'
While oranges chuckled with a jovial glow.

'Here's a taste of happiness!' papayas cried,
As we nibbled fruit, side by side.
Raspberries squealed, 'We're sweet like pie!'
While lemons just squirted, oh my, oh my!

In every morsel, joy would arrive,
As we chewed through laughter, feeling alive.
With each juicy bite, we couldn't resist,
Savoring slices of pure, fruity bliss.

Raindrops on Ripened Skin

In the garden, laughter flies,
Tomatoes giggle, oh what a prize!
Cucumbers dance in the summer sun,
While peppers shout, 'Aren't we fun?'

A watermelon rolls, faking a pout,
While berries tease, 'Come on, let's sprout!'
The beets wear shades, looking so cool,
As radishes whisper, 'Who's the fool?'

The Essence of Togetherness

Bananas slip on their zestful dreams,
Oranges huddle, sharing puckered schemes.
Apples and pears toss jokes in the air,
In this fruit fam, good vibes everywhere!

Grapes crack jokes about ending in wine,
While cherries giggle, 'Aren't we divine?'
This bowl of sillies, alive with delight,
Unites all flavors, oh what a sight!

Picking Moments from the Past

Plucked memories hang like ripe cherries bright,
Each bite brings a chuckle, a wink, pure delight.
Pineapples grin, recalling old tales,
While figs laugh at how they once sailed!

The apple recalls a butterfly's dance,
While the orange remembers a summer romance.
It's a juicy reunion, with giggles galore,
As fruits swap stories, always wanting more!

A Feast of Fleeting Hours

Banana splits under the bright moon's glow,
Peaches twirl 'round, putting on a show.
A potluck of laughter, a sprinkle of glee,
With fruit punch comments, oh so carefree!

Fleeting hours blend in a fizzy delight,
As time takes a nibble, it just feels right.
With each berry burst, memories ignite,
A banquet of chuckles, shining so bright!

Nature's Tender Hand

In the garden where gnomes play,
Tomatoes twirl in bright ballet.
Carrots dance with leafy grace,
As radishes make a silly face.

The apples giggle up in trees,
While strawberries laugh in the breeze.
A pumpkin winks with a big grin,
Inviting mice for a merry spin.

Sunflowers sway with joyful cheer,
Tickled by whispers that they hear.
Nature's hand, a gentle tease,
With every pluck, it aims to please.

So here's to life, in all its quirks,
Where veggies teach and nature works.
A light-hearted laugh, what a delight,
In this verdant realm, everything's right.

Threads of Laughter in Bloom

In the orchard, fruit is wise,
Peaches peek with twinkling eyes.
Cherries giggle, oh so sweet,
As plums tap dance on their feet.

A grapevine weaves a funny plot,
Bouncing around like a happy tot.
With every bloom, a chuckle fades,
Frantic flowers join the charades.

Bananas slip with jocular flair,
Jumping jovially without a care.
Melons join the pie dance spree,
Slicing jokes as they flee.

In this patch of leafy dreams,
Laughter bursts at the seams.
Every fruit, a humor craze,
Edible jokes in sunny rays.

Echoes of Autumn's Kiss

The leaves are laughing, yellow and red,
Cracking jokes as they fall from bed.
Squirrels scurry with acorns grand,
While pumpkins smile across the land.

Apples in baskets plot a prank,
Juicy jokes at the cider tank.
Cinnamon whispers lighten the air,
With each bite, surprise and flair.

A scarecrow tells tales in the field,
Hats flipped over, laughter is revealed.
Corn stalks sway with stories to share,
As critters gather without a care.

In this season, mirth is spun,
With every harvest, giggles run.
Autumn's kiss, a cheeky thing,
In nature's jokes, the heart does sing.

Embracing the Bloom

Blossoms chatter in the sun,
Tickled pink, oh what fun!
Bees buzzing in a lively hum,
Each petal dances, a burst of drum.

Daisies play peek-a-boo in rows,
With every bloom, a new joke grows.
Butterflies giggle in the light,
Waltzing on wings, a charming sight.

Tulips tease with a flirty sway,
While violets giggle, come what may.
Colors clash, a wild affair,
As laughter lingers in the air.

In the garden of jests and cheer,
Every fragrance whispers near.
Embracing the joys, sweet and bright,
In this tapestry of pure delight.

www.ingramcontent.com/pod-product-compliance
Lightning Source LLC
Chambersburg PA
CBHW070309120526
44590CB00017B/2597